1st Recital Series

FOR Bb TRUMPET

including works of:
- James Curnow
- Craig Alan
- Mike Hannickel
- Timothy Johnson
- Ann Lindsay

Solos for Beginning
through Early Intermediate
level musicians

CURNOW® MUSIC

EXCLUSIVELY DISTRIBUTED BY

HAL•LEONARD® CORPORATION

7777 W. BLUEMOUND RD. P.O. BOX 13819 MILWAUKEE, WI 53213

Edition Number: CMP 0687.02

1st Recital Series
Solos for Beginning through Early Intermediate level musicians
Trumpet

ISBN: 90-431-1677-7

CD Accompaniment tracks performed by Becky Shaw

CD number: 19.025-3 CMP

Foreword

High quality solo/recital literature that is appropriate for performers playing at the Beginner through Early Intermediate skill levels is finally here! Each of the **1st RECITAL SERIES** books is loaded with exciting and varied solo pieces that have been masterfully composed or arranged for your instrument.

Included with the solo book is a professionally recorded CD that demonstrates each piece. Use these examples to help develop proper performance practices. There is also a recording of the accompaniment alone that can be used for performance (and rehearsal) when a live accompanist is not available. A separate Piano Accompaniment book is available [edition nr. CMP 0753.02].

Table of Contents

☐   *Solo with accompaniment*

■   *Accompaniment*

1. ANTHEM

Mike Hannickel (ASCAP)

2. EVENING SHADOWS Timothy Johnson (ASCAP)

Bb TRUMPET

Johannes Brahms
3. HUNGARIAN DANCE # 5

Arr. **James Curnow** (ASCAP)

Bb TRUMPET

4. PROCESSION OF HONOR

Timothy Johnson (ASCAP)

Bb TRUMPET

5. ANCIENT TOWERS

Craig Alan (ASCAP)

6. COPPER AND ZINC

Ann Lindsay (ASCAP)

7. ROZINANTE

Mike Hannickel (ASCAP)

8. EXCURSION

Timothy Johnson (ASCAP)

Moderately (♩ = 96)

Jeremiah Clarke

9. TRUMPET VOLUNTARY

Arr. **Ann Lindsay** (ASCAP)

10. THE BRITISH GRENADIERS

Traditional
Arr. **James Curnow** (ASCAP)

Copyright © 2002 by **Curnow Music Press, Inc.**

11. BONNY DOON

James Miller
Arr. **Ann Lindsay** (ASCAP)

Bb TRUMPET

12. IN A FRENCH CAFE

Mike Hannickel (ASCAP)

Fast and happily (♩ = 108)